LOOKING **BACK**

HOLIDAYS AND PASTIMES

PHILIP SAUVAIN

Wayland

LOOKING BACK

CLOTHES AND FASHION

FAMILY LIFE

FOOD

HOLIDAYS AND PASTIMES

TRANSPORT

WORK

Series and Book editor: Rosemary Ashley
Designer: Bruce Low

First published in 1991 by
Wayland (Publishers) Limited
61 Western Road, Hove
East Sussex, BN3 1JD, England

British Library Cataloguing in Publication Data

Sauvain, Philip
Holidays and pastimes. – (Looking back)
I. Title   II. Series
790.09

ISBN 0–7502–0133–9

Typeset by DP Press Limited
Printed in Italy by G Canale C.S.p.A., Turin
Bound in Belgium by Casterman S.A.

CONTENTS

INTRODUCTION

The holidays and leisure activities enjoyed by our great-grandparents at the beginning of this century were very different from those enjoyed today. Most people had little time for leisure and life was very hard. Few families had holidays, and not many people watched or took part in sport. Many children went out to work when they were twelve years old and, for them, work was more important than play.

Our great-grandparents had no television or radio. But they entertained themselves with games, in the street or in the home, and sometimes with concerts, charades and singsongs. Rich people went to parties, balls and country-house weekends. For the poor, there might be the occasional travelling circus or day-trip to the seaside. But most poor people had no holidays at all, and many often spent what little free time they had in the chapel or at the pub.

The daily life of their great-grandchildren today is very

In the early years of the century, before the days of records, radio or television, people would 'make' their own music.

different. Most workers now have paid holidays each year. They work a five-day week and earn much higher pay. Many more people have the time and money to spend on hobbies and pastimes. They can watch television and listen to tapes and records. Some enjoy gardening, motoring or car maintenance. Many jog, walk, swim, climb, sail or cycle for fun. Their great-grandparents could do none of these things.

The holidays and pastimes we enjoy today came about for a number of reasons. Cheaper cars and huge passenger planes have made it possible for people to take holidays which they could only dream about in the past. The invention of radio, television, record players and computers has meant that people now have many different ways of spending their leisure time.

In the 1930s, portable gramophones allowed people to listen to music anywhere.

Windsurfing is a popular sport.

1 EARLY YEARS

At the beginning of the century the gap between rich and poor was very wide. In the city the family of an unskilled worker existed on his weekly earnings of around £1.1s (£1.05p). It is not surprising that such families could not afford a trip even to the neighbouring countryside.

Poor city children played street games. As families of ten or more children were quite usual, there was never a shortage of playmates. There was little danger from traffic, and always the chance of seeing a street entertainer, such as the Punch and Judy man or the organ grinder with his monkey. A Cockney woman talked about her youth. 'We used to have lots of dancing,' she said. 'Sometimes in the street, when the old barrel organ came round, especially on Saturdays after we had a beer or two.' In those days the pubs were open all day, and a pint of beer or tot of gin cost less than the price of a small bag of sweets. If some people spent most of their free

An organ grinder, with his monkey, plays his barrel organ in a London street.

time in the pub it was probably to forget how dreary their lives were at home.

Most towns had a music hall and a theatre. Music halls, especially, were hugely popular and the cheapest seats cost only a few pence. Shows consisted of 'variety' performances by comedians, singers, dancers, conjurors and other entertainers.

People in the countryside enjoyed simple pleasures, such as the annual village treat.

'The Choir Outing left in the small hours of the morning for Bournemouth or Weston-super-Mare; and the Children's School Treat Outing went, waving flags and singing, in a horse wagonette to the vicarage paddock in a neighbouring village, where tea and buns were partaken of at a long trestle table under some trees. After tea they ran races and played games, and returned home, tired and grubby, but still noisy, to find even a larger crowd than had seen them off waiting on the green to welcome them and join in their Hip-hip-hooray!'

From *Lark Rise to Candleford*, Flora Thompson

Edwardians enjoying a bank holiday trip to the seaside in 1902.

At Christmas there were pantomimes. Travelling entertainments, such as the circus, toured the country towns. A Norfolk woman remembered how she looked forward to the 'twice yearly fairs', in March and September. 'The galloping horses [roundabouts], swings, coconut shies and glaring lights caused great excitement,' she recalled.

Even in 1900 there were signs of changes to come. The newly-invented 'movies' were already popular. These early silent films lasted only a few minutes.

A visit to a fun-fair was a memorable day out for many people in the 1900s.

The flickering images on the screen were nicknamed 'flicks'. People watched them in travelling cinemas set up in tents, in converted shops and in music halls.

The first real cinema was opened in 1907. Soon every town had its *Picturedrome* or *Electric Palace*. The writer J.B. Priestley went to the *Theatre-de-Luxe* in Bradford. 'For sixpence [2½p] you were given an hour or so of short films, a cup of tea and a biscuit. I tried it once and once was enough,' he wrote. By 1914 it was reported that 'more people go to these places than to the theatres. Not only adults, but children, swarm to them night after night in large numbers.'

The Electric Theatre at Oxford.

A football match in 1914.

> A Norfolk woman recalled her holidays in 1910.
> *'There were excursions from Norwich to Yarmouth for one shilling and sixpence [7½p] on Bank Holidays, but we never patronised these, as the long steam trains were crammed to bursting, and the passengers were often boisterous and the worse for drink.*
>
> *We loved Gorleston . . . On the beach there was Punch and Judy and sometimes a pierrot show. Yarmouth, reached by a trip for sixpence in the river steamer, had more sophisticated pleasures, slot machines on Britannia Pier, and a photographer on the promenade who produced small dark photographs on a kind of tin backing.'*
>
> From *Within Living Memory*, The Boydell Press

More and more men also watched or took part in sport. Workers at the pit or mill finished at 1.00 pm on Saturdays, and watched the game – soccer, rugby league or cricket – in the afternoon. As yet, holidays away from home were only for the few. Most working people could not afford to stay in lodgings at a seaside resort. But on bank holidays they would travel by train on cheap day-trips to seaside towns like Blackpool, Brighton and Margate. Meanwhile, many of the middle classes and the very rich enjoyed a life of leisure. They dined out, went to the theatre and to parties and balls. They spent weekends at country houses, and were waited on by armies of servants. They played party games and hunted, and the men went out shooting and fishing.

Wealthy Edwardians enjoy a game of table tennis at a country-house party.

2 RELIEF FROM THE WAR

The First World War (fought against Germany) began for Britain on 4 August 1914, the day after August Bank Holiday. People remembered it well. A London woman remembered: 'the news was eagerly discussed by parties sitting on the beach, watching the children paddling and building castles.' People who had gone on holiday to Europe rushed back. They were packed like sardines in the trains and boats returning to Britain.

The war soon had an effect on most types of entertainment. Soccer players who joined the army even formed a 'Footballers' Battalion'. Music halls recruited volunteers for the army with patriotic songs, such as *Oh! It's a lovely war*, and *Pack up your troubles in your old kit bag*. Leading stars urged young men to come forward and volunteer. When they stepped on to the stage, the audience gave them a round of applause.

Musical comedies and variety shows helped to amuse wartime audiences.

In 1915 a writer on *The Times* described the first summer holiday of the War.

'From Hastings to Bognor the hotels and lodging houses are full. There are bands playing, and singers singing, the theatres and cinematographs are doing well, and every place has its little troupes of Funs or Drolls or Merries [entertainers], giving open-air entertainments.

At Brighton and everywhere else the crowd is quiet, all except the children. Mother, seeing them happy, is content to write to their father, who is maybe somewhere over the water, or in London, taking no holiday this year.'

Quoted in *Human Documents of the Lloyd George Era*, edited by E. Royston Pike

By 1916, after hundreds of thousands of soldiers had been killed or wounded in the fighting, people began to take a different view. One woman recalled, 'the amusement trade suffered, for by now many people were in mourning.' Instead there were patriotic concerts in the village hall 'to which we went accompanied by our knitting [clothes for soldiers].'

Life was confusing for the soldier on leave. He might enjoy the bright lights of the city one night and be back in the trenches of northern France the next night. 'Enjoy life while you can' was the motto of many young people. Over 150 new night clubs opened in London's West End in 1915 to meet the demand.

Dancing was popular in every town. Soldiers and war workers danced to the latest ragtime hits from America. These included *Alexander's Ragtime Band* and *Everybody's Doing It*. The cinema, too, helped people forget the war. 'Every picture-palace is crowded night after night', wrote a journalist in 1917. 'Some people visit different halls three or four times a week.'

Public houses did good business when the soldiers came on leave.

Mary Pickford was a famous screen star during the First World War.

The war also changed sports and games. The Olympic Games planned to take place in the German capital, Berlin, in 1916 were cancelled. Part of the Grandstand at the famous Ascot race course became a hospital.

The war also altered toys, games and books. Children now played 'war games' with toy soldiers and aircraft and they read comics which made fun of the German Kaiser (Emperor). There was even a pinball game called *Bitter pills for Kaiser Bill*. The player had to get the red, white and blue balls into the Kaiser's mouth.

Street parties celebrating the end of the war were held all over Britain.

3 THE RADIO AGE

Another sign of future change came soon after the war, with the first radio broadcast in 1920. Three years later, in 1923, listeners could tune in to daily broadcasts from 2LO – the BBC's London Radio Station. The day's programme began at 3.00 in the afternoon with light music. Then came children's stories and the news at 7.00 and again at 9.30 at night. Broadcasting ended with a dance band from a nightclub.

Listening to the wireless in the early days of broadcasting.

The wireless was a boon to those who lived alone or in the country. Many people spent their free time at home now instead of going to the pub. They listened to music and plays. They got the latest news without leaving the comfort of their living room.

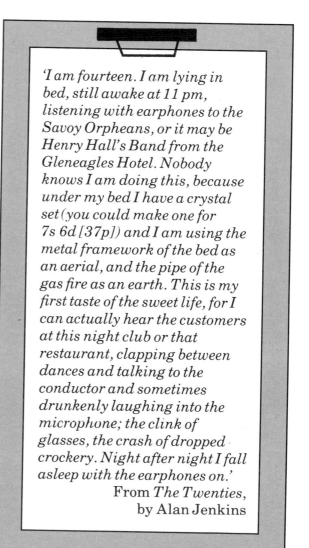

'I am fourteen. I am lying in bed, still awake at 11 pm, listening with earphones to the Savoy Orpheans, or it may be Henry Hall's Band from the Gleneagles Hotel. Nobody knows I am doing this, because under my bed I have a crystal set (you could make one for 7s 6d [37p]) and I am using the metal framework of the bed as an aerial, and the pipe of the gas fire as an earth. This is my first taste of the sweet life, for I can actually hear the customers at this night club or that restaurant, clapping between dances and talking to the conductor and sometimes drunkenly laughing into the microphone; the clink of glasses, the crash of dropped crockery. Night after night I fall asleep with the earphones on.'
From *The Twenties*,
by Alan Jenkins

Streets were still the main playgrounds for many children in the 1920s.

All through the 1920s and 1930s home leisure activities grew in importance as houses and flats became more pleasant places in which to live. The newer homes in the suburbs had gardens where children played, instead of in the streets. Families were smaller now, with fewer children. Most people had some money to spend in their free time. They bought cheap books and newspapers. Some collected stamps or cigarette cards. Papers like the *Daily Mirror* had competitions they could enter. One of the most popular was the crossword puzzle, which first appeared in the *Sunday Express* in 1924. Football pools, too, began in the 1920s.

People took a growing interest in popular music. In 1921 you could buy the first portable gramophone (record player). It used a steel needle to play heavy black records. They broke if you dropped them and each side only lasted three or four minutes. This

A 1920s 'flapper' plays the latest jazz records on her new gramophone.

'We went to the Zoo of all places. It was really most amusing. I hadn't been for ages and thoroughly enjoyed it. The bears and monkeys were divine. In the evening Phil and I went to an awfully good dance at the town hall . . . The people were all right and the supper excellent, with ices and claret cup and éclairs. The band was large but none too good. On the whole, however, it was one of the best I've been to this holiday.'

A diary entry written by Evelyn Waugh in 1920, From *The Diaries of Evelyn Waugh*

was long enough to play the tunes of the day.

Meanwhile the popularity of the music hall declined as that of the cinema grew. Luxurious new cinemas were opened in many towns, like the Granada Cinema, Tooting, in South London.

Young factory workers enjoy a day out at the seaside in 1925.

Going to the 'flicks' was a cheap and enjoyable form of entertainment. Films helped people to escape into a more exciting and glamorous world, and they became even more exciting when the first 'talkies' were screened in 1927.

Crowds still flocked to the seaside on bank holidays. In August 1926 a writer on the *Daily Mirror* said that 'not a room was to be had anywhere' in Southend. 'Night found at least 10,000 people sleeping on the beach and cliffs.' Many more people took

In spite of unemployment, more people could afford a visit to the zoo than would have been possible twenty years earlier.

In 1938 life was comfortable and pleasurable for the middle classes.

holidays away from home despite the growing numbers of unemployed. They often went to the same resorts as their friends. Asa Milton, a Blackburn teacher on holiday in the Isle of Man, wrote this in his diary in 1936: 'Such crowds, we never thought the ship would accommodate all, but it did and sailed away at 4.10. Wondered what sort of a crossing the Blackburn folk would have.'

In the 1920s less than two million people had a holiday each year with pay. In 1938 Parliament passed a new law, the Holidays with Pay Act, which gave every worker that right. By 1939 the number of people entitled to a holiday with pay had risen to over eleven million.

4 FORGETTING THE WAR

The radio broadcast news as well as entertainment. Millions listened to Winston Churchill's wartime speeches during the darkest days of the Second World War.

The Second World War began in September 1939. For the first time people at home were in the front line. The blackout each night and the air-raids each day changed the ways in which people spent their free time. Air-raids stopped play at cricket. The Women's League of Health and Beauty exercised in gas masks. A number of golf courses, cricket and football pitches were dug up to grow food.

Most people spent their free time at home. They listened to the wireless to keep up to date with the news. The wireless also kept them amused with shows like *ITMA*. This was first broadcast eight days after the start of war. It starred Tommy Handley and made fun of Hitler, the ruler of Germany and Britain's main enemy. *Workers' Playtime* and *Garrison Theatre* were other shows which were popular in the war years. Most people who lived through that time can still remember it to this day.

MAY 1943: *'I was ten when I stayed with my grandmother in a boarding house in Southport. We used to get scrambled eggs for breakfast. This was a wartime dish made from powdered eggs. It was awful. It had a revolting taste. We couldn't eat it. But we couldn't leave it on our plates, either, since there was a war on. Posters told you not to waste food. So we scooped it into a paper bag and buried it on the beach.'*
A Cheshire woman in 1990, recalling a wartime holiday.

Taking part in sport was also popular but some people felt guilty at first. They did not think it right to have fun when others were fighting. But they soon realized that soldiers and war workers had to relax as well as work. As in the First World War, they often did so in the dance hall.

Popular music cheered people up with songs like *Roll Out the Barrel* and *Run Rabbit Run*. In 1940 the BBC began to broadcast *Music While You Work* twice a day for factory workers. The singer Vera Lynn was known as 'The Forces' Sweetheart.' Concert parties played to the troops. In spite of the air raids, most of London's theatres managed to put on plays and shows in the war, but only one, the Windmill Theatre, stayed open all the time.

The popular singer Vera Lynn broadcasts to the forces serving overseas.

JULY 1943: 'As soon as we got off the train at the station [Hunstanton, Norfolk], we heard a woman telling her son, 'Breathe in Brian!' The signs of war were everywhere. The pier was closed and so were many of the hotels. There was barbed wire on the beach and on the cliffs. The town seemed full of men and women in uniform and there were lots of Americans about. I remember sitting on the cliffs gazing at the sky. Hundreds of bombers droned overhead heading out across the coast. It was only much later that I realized they were probably going to bomb a German city'.

Ian, who was a schoolboy during the Second World War, interviewed in 1990.

'Going to the pictures' was one of the chief ways of relaxing during the war. The Government closed the cinemas at the start of the war in 1939 but re-opened them a week later. They showed newsreels and films which were often planned to help the war effort. During one air-raid, a cinema manager told the audience that the warning siren had sounded and informed them they could get their money back. 'Few moved, I can tell you,' recalled a woman who worked in London at the time. 'Who cared if a bomb did drop. One would go out happy!'

Travel problems hit most people hard. Posters asked 'Is your journey *really* necessary? Train services were cut and petrol

For a few hours, dancing took everyone's thoughts away from the war.

In 1944, a boy makes sandpies on a safe, unmined part of the beach.

rationing made it almost impossible for drivers to use their cars for pleasure.

Visits to the seaside were rare because beaches had been mined and barricaded with barbed wire to prevent the Germans landing. Rows of poles had been placed in lakes to stop enemy sea planes from landing.

5 AFTER THE WAR

When the war ended in 1945, going to the cinema was still a popular pastime. In small towns it was often the only place to go at night other than the pubs. Many people went to the 'pictures' two or three times a week. But the boom did not last. By the early 1950s many people were staying at home. They were watching television instead. Sales of TV sets increased sharply at the time of the Queen's Coronation in 1953, and again in 1955 when independent television first started.

It was a great novelty, in the 1950s, to watch moving pictures as well as listen to sound, in one's own sitting room.

Because of the competition from television, theatres and cinemas soon began to close. But the film industry fought back. It tried to tempt audiences with special wide-screen films made in *Cinemascope* and *Cinerama*. These gave people the chance to see a spectacular film in colour on a huge wide screen, instead of watching a small black and white picture on television.

But other entertainments besides television were also keeping people at home. In the

Many young people enjoyed listening to pop records, played on juke boxes in coffee bars in the 1950s and '60s.

'Television was still a novelty then [1953] and I was only 14. I'd never seen it before and wasn't likely to, since we didn't have electricity on the farm. I was dying to know what all the fuss was about. My chance came when I went to stay with a friend in Barnsley. I don't remember much about it except the family sitting with their eyes glued to a tiny screen. The set itself was quite bulky and took up a lot of space. It was black and white, of course. Colour didn't come in for many years.'

A farmer's daughter interviewed in 1990

1950s, record players took the place of the old portable gramophones. The new lighter, plastic records were stronger and less likely to break. They revolved at slower speeds. The sound was better and each LP (long player) could play for over twenty minutes a side instead of only three or four minutes. LPs were followed ten years later by stereo records which sounded even better through a pair of loudspeakers.

23

Holidaymakers enjoying themselves at a holiday camp in the 1950s.

Seaside holidays in Britain became very popular in the years just after the war. Most people had better-paid jobs now. There was little unemployment and most workers were able to enjoy annual holidays with pay. Some went abroad in the 1950s but most stayed in Britain.

Many went to the holiday camps which Billy Butlin opened at Skegness and Filey and at other resorts around the coast. These camps gave people the chance to enjoy a week's holiday at a price they could afford. Everything was included.

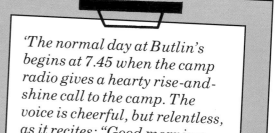

'The normal day at Butlin's begins at 7.45 when the camp radio gives a hearty rise-and-shine call to the camp. The voice is cheerful, but relentless, as it recites: "Good morning, campers. It is a lovely day and the sun is shining (or, the weather has let us down) so show a leg you lads and lasses, rub the sleep out of your eyes and prepare for another grand day of fun, another Butlin's jolliday." '

Life in a Holiday Camp,
Picture Post, 13 July 1946

A visitor said campers were 'expected to take part each morning in army style keep-fit exercises. They do so. And they like it.' Butlin said the secret of his success was that he gave the campers what they wanted. 'They come back year after year. That is my test.'

By 1960, however, many people were using their cars to take caravans and tents to the seaside. Many others went to the lakes and mountains of northern England, Scotland and Wales.

Those who went on day-trips to the coast in their cars, often went elsewhere for their annual holidays. Many holidaymakers went abroad. By now there were travel agents in most towns. They sold package holidays to the hot and sunny coasts of Spain and Italy. Cheap air travel made dreams come true. Charter flights could take tourists to the Spanish beaches of Benidorm and Torremolinos for little more than the cost of a seaside holiday in Britain.

Cheaper air fares meant that people could travel as far away as Australia.

6 IN RECENT YEARS

Since 1960 the leisure industry has grown by leaps and bounds. One of the biggest changes has been in pop music. The Saturday night dance at the local ballroom was packed with dancers thirty years ago. You could dance the quickstep and the waltz there and jive to music with a stronger beat. A writer described jivers with their skirts swirling and coat tails flying. 'They throw each other away, then, magnetized, come together,' he said.

A dance hall in the 1960s, packed with dancers doing the 'twist'.

A Yorkshire woman remembered ballroom dancing in the 1960s
'I can see them now – the Locarno, Wakefield, and the Locarno, Bradford – with their neon signs and the dancers queuing outside. You got quite excited as you neared the door since you could hear the music as people went in. They had terrific bands in those days with about ten or a dozen musicians in matching suits, and a singer.

Some of the crowd used to stand in front of the band to watch. But most people got up to dance and twist – except the crowd of men standing near the exit. By ten o'clock it was so packed, you couldn't dance properly at all. You were squashed tight against the other people on the dance floor. You moved when they moved. If you wanted to go out, the people at the box office stamped your hand so you could get back in.'

Pop music began in the 1950s. It continues to entertain and influence the lifestyle of generations of young people.

Jiving was followed by rock 'n' roll and the twist. The rock 'n' roll years began with Bill Haley and the Comets and their hit record *We're Gonna Rock Around the Clock* in 1954. The demand for pop music grew as disc jockeys played the same records over and over again on the radio. Millions watched television programmes like *Juke Box Jury* and *Top of the Pops*. One result of all this publicity was that young people wanted to dance to their favourite pop records. Discotheques and disc jockeys took the place of the Saturday night dance.

There were new ways of playing music in the home as well. Children learned to play the guitar and the electronic keyboard.

The coming of colour television in 1966, made the TV set the centre of entertainment in the home. By 1990 many people had video-cassette recorders as well. They used them to play back movies hired from a video shop or recorded from television. Despite this the cinema survived. Many of the huge luxurious cinema buildings were divided into smaller cinemas so that several films could be shown at once. Spectacular new films brought back the crowds, such as *Superman*, *Jaws*, *Star Wars* and *Batman*.

Keeping fit has recently become a way of life. From jogging to weight training, from aerobics to dance, the message is that fitness is important for health, as well as being a lot of fun. There are lots of different ways to become or stay fit – in fact, there are almost as many ways as there are people. Whatever your favourite sporting activity – be it horse-riding or callanetics, skiing or badminton – there are sure to be facilities available to you.

From *Fitness* by Kate Haycock, 1990

Football continues to be hugely popular with large numbers of people.

Many people enjoy the exciting sport of hang gliding.

Many people were earning high salaries and could afford to spend two or three weeks abroad for their annual holiday. The growth of air transport, with huge 'jumbo' planes, has meant that previously undreamt of visits to such places as the USA, Thailand, the Caribbean islands and Kenya were becoming commonplace.

People found new ways to relax. Plenty could now afford to have a night out in a restaurant or a nightclub. Thirty years earlier their parents would have gone to a dance or to the pictures instead.

Many more people now enjoyed sports and new sports became popular, such as water skiing, hang gliding, roller disco, windsurfing, skateboarding and skiing. Towns built sports centres and Olympic-sized swimming pools. Keeping fit became a pastime for many and people practised yoga, jogging, marathon running and aerobics.

'There are two types of people in Britain today,' said a teacher in 1990. 'The watchers who spend all their time in front of the telly and the doers who get up and go!' Whether people enjoy watching plays and films or other people's sports on television, or, themselves, take part in one of the hundreds of different sports available, they are enjoying pastimes and taking holidays in ways undreamt of by their great-grandparents.

Nowadays, jogging is popular as a sport and for physical fitness.

GLOSSARY

Aerobics Exercises designed to make the heart beat faster.

Callanetics A course of carefully worked out exercises to tone up the muscles.

Charter flight An aircraft hired out to make a special journey, such as one taking people on holiday to a foreign airport.

Cinemascope Extra-wide cinema screen process first used in 1953 in *The Robe*.

Cinerama Extra-wide cinema screen process introduced in the early 1950s. It used three projectors running at the same time to show a film.

Crystal set Early type of wireless set. You listened to it through earphones.

Flapper A name given to young, modern women in the 1920s.

Football pools A nationwide pastime of betting on the results of football matches.

ITMA A very popular radio programme during the Second World War. ITMA stood for *It's That Man Again*.

Jiving Jerky American dance of the 1940s and 1950s. Performed to music with a strong beat, such as jazz or rock 'n' roll.

Organ grinder The person who played a barrel organ – an instrument that produced music by the turning of a handle. A pet monkey often sat on top of the barrel organ.

Package holiday An all-inclusive holiday organised by a tour company and paid for in advance.

Pierrot shows Entertainments with clowns.

Ragtime Early type of jazz. It was often played on the piano.

Trenches Long, deep ditches used for the protection of troops during the First World War.

Twist Popular dance of the 1960s in which dancers twisted their hips in time to rock and roll music.

2LO The London radio station of the BBC in the early 1920s.

Volunteers People who offered their services in the armed forces during the two world wars.

PICTURE ACKNOWLEDGEMENTS

Aquarius 12 (top); Mary Evans 9 (lower), 11, 13, 14, 15 (top), 17; Hulton Pictures cover, 4, 7, 8 (both), 10, 15 (lower), 16, 18, 19, 20, 21, 23; Billie Love Collection 12 (lower), 25; Mansell Collection 5 (top), 6; Peter Newark 8 (top); Topham Picture Library 5 (lower), 22, 24, 26, 27, 28, 29 (both).

IMPORTANT DATES

1907 The Balham Empire, Britain's first cinema, opened in London
1908 Olympic Games held in London
1914 Outbreak of First World War
1922 Regular broadcasting by the BBC's 2LO station began
1923 First FA Cup Final at Wembley Stadium
1927 First talking pictures seen and heard in Britain
1936 First regular television broadcasts in Britain
1938 Holidays with Pay Act passed by Parliament
1939 Outbreak of Second World War
1946 BBC Television started again after the War
1948 Olympic Games held in London
1955 Independent Television (ITV) began
1966 First colour television service began

BOOKS TO READ

Finding Out About Edwardian Britain by Michael Rawcliffe (Batsford 1989)
How We Used To Live, 1902–1926 by Freda Kelsall (A & C Black, 1985)
How We Used To Live, 1954–1970 by Freda Kelsall (A & C Black, 1987)
Young in the Twenties by Eleanor Allen (A & C Black, 1988)

Books about individual decades
The Forties and Fifties by Nathaniel Harris (Macdonald, 1975)
The Sixties by Nathaniel Harris (Macdonald, 1975)
The Seventies by John Edwards (Macdonald, 1980)
The Eighties by Edward Grey (Wayland, 1989)

ACKNOWLEDGEMENTS

Quotations on the following pages are reprinted by kind permission of: Oxford University Press, from *Lark Rise to Candleford* by Flora Thompson, page 7; Rainbird Publishing Group, from *The Twenties* by Alan Jenkins, page 13; Weidenfeld and Nicolson, from *The Diaries of Evelyn Waugh* by Evelyn Waugh page 15.

INDEX